Pan Gu Mystical Qigong

Pan Gu Mystical Qigong

Ou Wen Wei

Multi-Media Books
Burbank, California

In Association With
Guangzhou Pan Gu Mystical Qigong
Research Association
Guangzhou University Qigong Science
Research Institute

First published in 1999 by Multi-Media Books, an imprint of Unique Publications, Inc.

LCCN:
ISBN: 1-892515-06-7

Distributed by:
Unique Publications
4201 Vanowen Place
Burbank, CA 91505
(800) 332-3330

First edition
05 04 03 02 01 00 99 98 97 1 3 5 7 9 10 8 6 4 2
Printed in the United States of America

Designed by Dino Flores
Edited by Mark V. Wiley

Take kindness and benevolence as basis;
Take frankness and friendliness as bosom.
Speak with reason; Treat with courtesy;
Move with emotion; Act with result.

—Ou Wen Wei

Table of Contents

1

Overview of
Pan Gu Mystical Qigong

Pan Gu Mystical Qigong (or the Heaven, Earth, Sun, and Moon Qigong) is a discipline that I originated through many years of extremely agonizing tempering, and through negotiation with a kind of supernatural power. I did this according to the characteristics of the physiological structure of the human body and the relationship between man and the Universe.

My academic thesis, "A Special Knowledge of Matter and Spiritual Characteristic Qigong," won the Gold Cup award in the "First Session of International Somatic Science Conference," held in the United States in June of 1995. At the same time, it was selected and compiled in the treatise of "The Fourth Session of International Qigong Science Congress."

I am currently the director of Guangzhou University Qigong Science Research Institute and president of the Guangzhou Pan Gu Mystical Qigong Research Association. I publicly presented Pan Gu Mystical Qigong for the first time in 1993. Since then, it has been well accepted by society at large. Pan Gu Mystical Qigong is now being propagated widely throughout the United States, as well as in Hong Kong, Macao, Indonesia, Australia,

Italy, Colombia, Panama, and Canada. Pan Gu Mystical Qigong has been received and mastered by hundreds of practitioners, making many of them who are plagued with the agony caused by sickness to regain their health and march toward new life.

The genesis of Pan Gu Mystical Qigong theory is captured in four principles. The first principle is to cure sickness and disease, save the patient, and bring happiness to mankind. The second principle is that of properly conducting oneself in society and the key of exercising Pan Gu Mystical Qigong. This is achieved through adhering to the following philosophy: "To take kindness and benevolence as its basis, to take frankness and friendliness as its bosom." The third principle is "to turn mystery into reality and to transform complexity into simplicity." The fourth principle reflects on the way of treating others and dealing with affairs. Its philosophy is: "To speak with reason, to treat people with courtesy, to move others with emotion, and to act with result."

Pan Gu Mystical Qigong is a special knowledge, possessing both matter and spiritual characteristics. The matter characteristic shows itself as a special energy, a special form of the molecular movement, a special kind of field. The spiritual characteristic mainly refers to the dynamic ability that surpasses matter characteristic and manifests itself in vitality and thinking ability. The spiritual characteristic has conscious action and super-conscious action. The relations between all things and matter in the universe—including man and man, man and matter, matter and matter—coexist while opposing one another, are tolerant then stable, are harmonious then resonant. The philosophical viewpoint of Pan Gu Mystical Qigong, then, is that of harmony prevailing among the Heaven, Earth, and man.

The contents of the mode (or practice) of Pan Gu Mystical Qigong is to absorb the cream of the sun and the moon and the essential qi of the universe, then use it to suppress the evil and to make known the merits, to help mankind and to guide its people. The principle of Pan Gu Mystical Qigong is formulated according to the dialectical relations that exist among and between various kinds of things and matter contained in the formation, development, and trend of the Heaven, Earth, and man.

Pan Gu Mystical Qigong has condensed the factors in the Universe that are beneficial to man and matter, and has provided the function of self-adjustment. As a result, if practitioners of this qigong form are willing to conduct themselves in the correct manner and to deal with things according to the principle of "taking kindness and benevolence as its basis, taking frankness and friendliness as its bosom," put forward by the qigong mode, and to insist on exercising according to the contents stipulated by the qigong mode, then the effect of curing sickness, strengthening body, developing wisdom, and living in harmony and friendship with others will be realized.

When the practitioners of this qigong form delve deep into the exercises and closely link with the theory of the mystical book *The Path of Life,* they can reach a wonderful realm wherein the Universe and man combine to form one and move toward the eternal human world.

The principles of curing sickness through Pan Gu Mystical Qigong are two. The first principle is that by performing the exercises outlined herein according to the rules, the practitioner will directly absorb the matter elements from the great nature that are beneficial to the human body, and will cure the sickness caused by the lack of the matter elements in the organs of the body. The second principle achieved through exercising is that the physiological function of the human body will be enhanced, thus curing the sickness caused by the obstruction of the physiological function in the organs of the body.

The trait of Pan Gu Mystical Qigong is simple and easy to learn in a short time, has a quick effect, needs no quietness to perform, there is no absorption needed or taboo inflicted, and it remains free from any conception of faction or school. It advocates the philosophy that "practice is the basis, comprehension is a short-cut" and that one must "take practice as the teacher and take society as the master to bring happiness to mankind."

The book you hold in your hands is a mystical, yet real narration, giving a full account of Pan Gu's opening of the Heaven and the Earth, the formation of the Universe, the coming into being of mankind, their marching into the future world, and the theoretical basis upon which this mystical qigong rests.

2

The Mode of
Pan Gu Mystical Qigong

Pan Gu Mystical Qigong aims at absorbing the essence of the sun and the moon and the real qi of the Chaos, so as to suppress the evil and to develop the good, to relieve the world and to help the people. The aim of this qigong form is to "take benevolence and kindheartedness as the basis; to take frankness and magnanimousness as the bosom; to make body and soul pleasant to strengthen and promote health; to warn the evil and to eliminate the wickedness; to relieve the world and to help the people."

What is unique about Pan Gu Mystical Qigong is that its movements are simple to practice, and are rich and plentiful in connotation. The practice easily brings out extraordinary function in the human body. Practitioners of this form will not be infatuated or spellbound during practice. Upon deeper penetration during practice, the practitioners are able to combine closely with the theory of the mystical book *The Path of Life*, supplementing practice and theory. As a result, practitioners will reach a wonderful realm featuring the combination and amalgamation of the Universe and man, so as to transit toward the eternal human world.

Pan Gu Mystical Qigong is divided into three levels, with three rounds in each level. Each round consists of motions to the left, right, and the middle, with twenty-six repetitions of each motion, each lasting about one second in duration. After finishing each level, the practitioner is to hold their palms upward, as if holding a chrysanthemum in their palms.

Practice Method

1. Starting Position

Stand naturally (those who feel uncomfortable standing may practice in a sitting position), with the width between two feet the same as that between two shoulders. Hold both of your hands naturally, with palms facing up in front of your waist, with fingers opened naturally. (Figure 1)

Once in this position, concentrate on your thoughts and close your eyes. Repeat three times in your head: "Take kindliness and benevolence as its basis, take frankness and friendliness as its bosom. This is the condition of receiving gong which lasts for six to ten minutes."

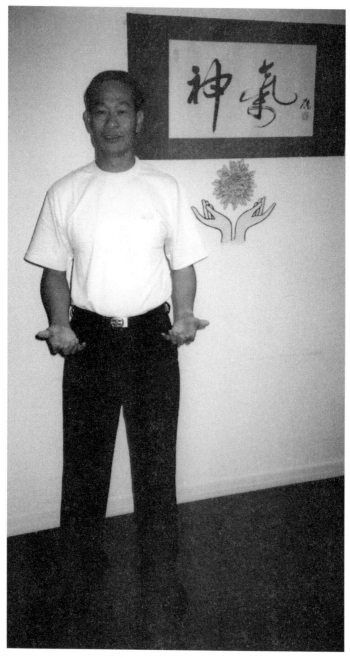

Figure 1

2. Left Side Motion

Move your left hand slightly to the right so that it is now held in front of your waist. Raise your right hand so that it is held above the left, with palm facing down and held parallel to the palm of your left hand. The distance between two hands is fifteen to twenty centimeters. (Figure 2)

Once in this position, imagine that you are holding the sun between your hands. Once you have this vision in your mind, intersect and rotate your hands clockwise twenty-six times while counting to yourself. When rotating the hands, the little finger must turn before others. (Figure 3)

Figure 2

Figure 3

3. Right Side Motion

Flip your hands so that your right hand is now held in front of your waist. Your left hand is held above the right, with palm facing down and held parallel to the palm of your right hand. The distance between two hands is fifteen to twenty centimeters. (Figure 4)

Once in this position, imagine that you are holding the moon between your hands. Once you have this vision in your mind, intersect and rotate your hands counter-clockwise twenty-six times while counting to yourself. When rotating the hands, the little finger must turn before others. (Figure 5)

Figure 4

Figure 5

4. Middle Motion

Rotate your hands until they are at their respective sides
and held parallel to each other. While maintaining this
position, raise your hands until they reach chest height.
The distance between the hands is fifteen-to-twenty centimeters. (Figure 6)

Once in this position, imagine you are kneading the sun
and the moon together, then intersect and turn your hands
clockwise in a forward direction twenty-six times while
counting to yourself. (Figure 7)

•   •   •

Repeat movements 1–4 in sequence a total of three times.
You have now completed the first level of exercising Pan
Gu Mystical Qigong.

Figure 6

Figure 7

28 • The Mode of Pan Gu Mystical Qigong

5. Drawing Open Motion

Once you have completed three sets of movements 1–4, straighten and slowly draw open your hands in front of your chest, while at the same time breathing deeply through your nose. (Figures 8–10)

Figure 8

Figure 9

Figure 10

The Mode of Pan Gu Mystical Qigong • 31

6. Drawing Close Motion

After fully expanding your arms, embrace the Universe with your hands before you. Do this by exhaling slowly through your nose, while at the same time slowly drawing your hands back in front of your chest. (Figures 11–12)

Figure 11

Figure 12

7. Chrysanthemum Pose

Following the open and close drawing motions, place your hands before your chest, forming and holding the chrysanthemum hand seal. (Figure 13)

• • •

Repeat movements 5–7 in sequence a total of three times. You have now completed the second level of exercising Pan Gu Mystical Qigong.

Figure 13

8. After finishing the above two levels, draw your hands back near your waist with palms facing up, and read in your heart: "Speak with reason, treat people with courtesy, move others with emotion and act with result." (Figure 14)

• • •

You have now completed the third level of exercising Pan Gu Mystical Qigong, thus concluding the exercise routine.

Figure 14

Guidelines for Practice

1. Exercise can be carried out wherever the exerciser feels comfortable and is free from fatigue. Time, place, and direction are not considerations for effective practice. Frequent practice will be more favorable toward curing disease and strengthening the body, as well as helping others in curing their diseases.

2. Read silently the key of the *gong* mode before exercising. The time for receiving *qi* is not set. It may take three-to-five minutes or ten-to-twenty minutes. When time is pressing, it may be exercised at once. Generally, six minutes is preferable.

3. It is advisable to exercise qigong in a standing pose, although patients may take a sitting or lying pose when necessary. If you are unable to turn your hands as directed, you can place one hand upward and the other downward, and imagine you are turning your hands.

4. There is no need of absorption, nor a specific practice of breathing, as these things have nothing to do with the main and collateral meridian channels of the body. Unconscious auto-moving qigong is also not encouraged. It makes no sense to become spellbound. Furthermore, not doing so may adjust those who have gone astray, or into deviation, as a result of having learned the mode or practice of other schools of qigong.

5. Count silently twenty-six times when exercising, one second per time. Sometimes a miscount may occur, but a more or less count is not a matter of importance; just stop when you find that the number is over twenty-six. It does not matter if you get the wrong number, but you should gradually make it accurate.

6. Provided that there are interruptions or phone calls during exercising, back-collecting of the *qi* is not needed. The exercisers may either continue the exercise after having dealt with the distractions, or do it from the beginning and be not a stickler for formalities.

7. Take it easy and be natural when exercising. It will not be harmful if the exerciser occasionally diverts attention.

8. The exercises will be effective whether the exerciser detects the feeling of *qi* or not. The so-called "feeling of *qi*," if it differs from the usual cool, numb, hot, swell, pain, etc., is a normal phenomenon.

9. The general requirement is to ask for something, yet not force yourself to ask for it. Ask for nothing, yet ask for everything. At last the exerciser is able to ask for everything. Diligence conditions success. When success emerges, nothing will be impossible. It has a profound significance.

10. The state of mind during exercising should be kind, peaceful, and broad.

11. Always bear the key of the *gong* mode in mind: "Take kindliness and benevolence as its basis; take frankness and friendliness as its bosom."

12. The exercisers should pay attention to the following five practices:

      1. The practice of exercising qigong: do it constantly and diligently everyday.

      2. The practice of reading: read the book *The Path of Life* earnestly and seriously to gain a deeper understanding, then an abrupt comprehension will come into being from gradual comprehension.

      3. The practice of treating illness: treat more patients. Take the agony of others as your own, even if you are sick. You may as well treat patients and help others. The greater your love, the greater your ability to heal.

      4. The practice of guiding people: propagate the Pan Gu Mystical Qigong so as to accumulate virtue and kindness.

5. The practice of conducting oneself: "take kindliness and benevolence as its basis, take frankness and friendliness as its bosom." This is the principle of conducting oneself in society, which is the most important. The exercisers should at all times look to the depths of their souls to examine their words and deeds and see whether there are shortcomings and errors. We must restrain ourselves and suit others.

13. Treat patients with three hearts: the heart of love, the heart of perseverance, and the heart of confidence.

14. As curative effects are obtained from treating others' diseases, which is due to self-effort and the reward of the mode of the *gong*, so we should be modest and prudent, and should by no means be proud and conceited. We should exercise more and read the book, so as to enhance and raise the energy and the ability of the qigong, to bring happiness to ourselves and to others.

15. Sometimes there may be indisposition during exercise. This is caused by the struggle between the essence air the exercisers inhale from the Heaven and the Earth and the sick air. So long as you persist in the exercise or increase the time of the exercise, indisposition will gradually turn for the better.

16. If people at some other places wish to learn this form of qigong, or they need to be cured and adjusted, but they cannot learn at once, you may teach them how to receive the *qi*.

17. The exercisers may see doctors and take medicines at the same time as practicing qigong without contradiction. But those who have been taking medicine and find a turn for the better after exercising qigong, may reduce the dose of the medicine gradually and stop taking it (with doctor's permission, of course!)

18. There are no taboos in menu and no commandments in everything.

19. There may appear pictures or sounds in your mind when exercising qigong, take no heed of it, don't be alarmed and panicky, nor pursue them.

20. Extraordinary functions of all kinds may be developed in exercising. Don't pursue them, but adopt a correct attitude toward them.

21. Don't teach others at random after you have learned the exercises to avoid losing the information and vitality and strength the teacher gave you.

22. After having learned moving qigong for two months, you can learn static qigong exercises.

23. Classes are sponsored by Master Ou. The subject of the lecture each time is different. They are helpful in enhancing the level of comprehension, the energy, and the ability of the qigong exercises, so more attendance is advisable.

24. The exercisers should constantly join in the region or group of activities. The activities are exercising qigong in groups, adjusting bodies mutually, inter-flowing experience of the *gong*-exercise and the comprehension in reading the book *The Path of Life*. All this will be helpful to the health and raising the ability of the qigong exercises.

25. Pan Gu Mystical Qigong is free from any conception of faction or school. Those who have learned and exercised other kinds of qigong may also exercise it. But it is preferable to exercise Pan Gu Mystical Qigong in a certain period for comparison so as to find out which practice suits you best.

26. There is a *qi* field in the student certificates and name cards of Master Ou. They are helpful in treating diseases. Please keep them carefully. (They will not be reissued if lost.) Only those who own the student certificates and Master Ou's name cards through attending a lecture or teaching by correspondence, are the regular students of the Pan Gu Mystical Qigong, and they will get best result and effect.

3

Theory and Evolution
Pan Gu Mystical Qigong

What is Pan Gu?

It was Pan Gu who is dealt with in the oldest myth in China. He was also the first to record Chinese history. Therefore, we often hear a rather proud phrase regarding him: "Since the opening of the Heaven and the Earth by Pan Gu, the three sovereigns and five emperors have been ruling until now."

From ancient times until today, the sages, men of virtue, and the common man, whenever there was a need to quote the classics or authoritative works, this phrase would be naturally quoted to describe the early opening of the Chaos and the beginning of the Heaven and the Earth. And this remark was also proudly quoted in the article "On the Tactics Against Japanese Imperialism," written by Mao Ze Dong.

There is a record found in *Tai Ping Imperial Reading: Three and Five Historical Narration*, which states: "The Heaven and the Earth were as chaotic as an egg. Pan Gu was born in it, eighteen thousand years elapsed. He opened the

Heaven and the Earth. The clear *yang* became the Heaven, and the turbid *yin* formed the Earth. Pan Gu was in it, and had nine changes in a day. The deity was in the Heaven, the sage was on the Earth. The Heaven became three-and-one-third meters higher every day, the Earth became three-and-one-third meters thicker everyday, and Pan Gu became three-and-one-third meters taller everyday. It lasted for eighteen-thousand years, so the Heaven was extremely high, Pan Gu was extremely tall. The Heaven and the Earth had thus a distance of ninety-thousand li."

The following vivid description can be found in *Five Yun Historical Record:* "Pan Gu was born first. When he was dying, his *qi* was transformed into wind and cloud, his voice into thunder, his left eye became the sun, his right eye became the moon, his four limbs and five bodies became the four polars and the five mountains, his blood was converted into the rivers and streams, his tendons and veins into the geography, his muscle into the field and the earth, his hair and beard into stars, his skin into trees and grasses, his teeth and bones into gold and stone, his marrow and pith into pearl and jade, his sweat into rain, the sperm in his body was touched by the wind and turned into the people at large."

These concise and comprehensive remarks afford food for thought. It is more imaginative and reasonable and more solemn and stirring than that narration regarding Genesis from the Western world. So long as you think about it carefully, you will find it not only gives a very vivid and concrete description on the time during, before, and after the opening of the Heaven and the Earth, but also deeply reveals the close relationship between Heaven, Earth, and man, and discloses extremely plain and profound philosophical reasoning.

The phrase, "The Heaven and the Earth were as chaotic as an egg," deals with the condition before the opening of the Heaven and the Earth. At that time the Universe was a dark, chaotic air mass that looked like an egg.

The phrase, "Pan Gu was born in it," deals with the fact

that there existed in it some matter which contained vitality, waiting to show the spirituality and force when the time matured. In these few words, there embodies vaguely the dialectical relation of the saying: "Life originated from the Universe and in turn would certainly act on the Universe." To express the view of the present people which can be easily comprehended, it will be read as: "The great nature nurses the man, and the man can also act on the great nature, to reform the environment of the great nature so as to make it better fit the need of man's life and will."

Thus, the phrase, "Eighteen-thousand years elapsed, he opened the Heaven and the Earth, the clear *yang* became the Heaven, while the turbid *yin* formed the Earth," means that Pan Gu, this biological substance, after eighteen-thousand years exerting himself, had accumulated enough energy, and was thus able to reform the natural environment around him according to his own will. So, he sifted the matter particles in the Chaos, letting the light and clear particles remain floating in the air, and the heavy and turbid ones accumulate to form the Earth (celestial body). The space thus became clear and bright and the arrangement of the matter looked in order and was no longer chaotic. The difference of the Heaven and the Earth was formed and the natural laws of various kinds which have been cognized by now or are beyond our cognizance were also constituted. As such, Pan Gu was able to create man and create things in a more planned way and in more proper step and measure. The argument revealed here is quite plain and easy to understand—which is as simple as we tidy up the room that had been at odds with disordered things—so as to live and work better.

The phrase, "The deity was in the Heaven, the sage was on Earth," deals with the fact that his spirit (which can be understood as the soul or the capacity of thought) could gallop freely and was as vast and agile as the sky; his body was as heavy and thick as the Earth; and he took the Earth as his standing basis. Therefore, he could "modify nine times within one day." This modification referred to the transformation of thought first—to think how to reform himself and the environment according to his own feature, his own ability and the actual condition of the environment in which he existed. Then Pan Gu managed to realize this modification of thought, making it become a new reality. So this transformation had its good ground and rules and was of the combination of subjective initiative and the objective condition which caused transformation of function. This is just like human beings of today, who need a close subjective and objective combination first, and then obtain the function in keeping their self-reformation, self-perfection, and creating wealth.

It will not be difficult to comprehend the description of how Pan Gu created things and bred man, as indicated in the *Five Yun Historical Record*, after having understood the above argument.

The phrase "Pan Gu was born first," describes the chaotic air mass, which looked like an egg, bred and bore the first living body that had subjective initiative: Pan Gu. It was really a great gain of the nature breeding and the crystallization of the highest sublimation caused by the accumulation of the boundless time and space with the cream of countless matter particles, representing the will of the originally disordered time and space. As a result, the disorderly matter particles began to shift their course toward orderly condition in their development. Thus, they bestowed a sacred mission on Pan Gu: a high-energy living body, bred and created by them together to open up the orderly time and space and to breed man and create things in order. Pan Gu realized this sacred mission and made up his mind to carry it out as his own responsibility, so the following description came into being:

"When he was dying, Pan Gu's *qi* was transformed into wind and cloud, his voice into thunder, his left eye into the sun, his right eye into the moon, . . . his muscle was converted into the field and the Earth . . . his teeth and bones into gold and stones . . . the sperm in his body was touched by the wind and turned into the people at large."

The sperm in Pan Gu's body carried the genetic factor of Pan Gu, combining the cream of things in order which had been transformed from his blood and flesh body that bred again mankind. Man, bred during this time, was not an individual but a group, so they should be called mankind. Then those people in turn bred their descendants and carried on in order, continuing the great breeding and creation of things, so as to make better and more reasonable arrangement and coexistence of time, space, and matter (particles) in the Universe. It was the real implication of the phrase, "Pan Gu opening the Heaven and the Earth," found in the most ancient myths. It was the real purpose of Pan Gu opening the Heaven and Earth, as well as the real aim in breeding Pan Gu together with time, space, and matter (particles) in the Universe.

Therefore, we may associate the theory and origin of Pan Gu with the theory of evolution. From the basic view of the theory of evolution, humans also evolved by time, space, and matter: the three essential elements in the specified condition of this Earth.

Looking on the surface of thing, the Earth seems to be the mother body of mankind; but in reality, the Universe is still the basic mother body! The Earth is only a little baby in the Universe. Judging from this obvious fact, human life originated from the Universe. The question which is worth thinking posits that: the theory of evolution, approved by modern science, is identical in many respects in content and in reason with the saying of Pan Gu opening the Heaven and the Earth and of his breeding mankind and creating things.

First came the breeding by nature. The "lifeless things" (the elements of matter or particles). They accumulated, sublimated, evolved, and became the senior living beings which had intelligence (the ability of thought) and which were endowed with a sacred mission: to reform the nature in order. This reformation should be carried on in conformity with the relation of the Heaven and the Earth (the law of the nature), otherwise it will be punished by the Heaven (namely calamity). The environmental pollution of today has mercilessly proved this to be so. As a result, the most important duty of mankind is to thoroughly understand the true features and the inner relationship of various things in the Heaven and the Earth (the Universe) so as to conform and make use of those relationships to reform the nature and to bring happiness to mankind. Only by doing so, can a more peaceful, better, and everlasting life be obtained.

The ancient philosophical thought regarding these questions has already had been put out dialectically. Harmony means combination, things coexist in tune and are very intimate with each other, conform to each other's characteristic, learn from and help each other to make up each other's deficiencies, do only the things which are beneficial to others, and never do things which are harmful to others. By doing so, they can more cooperatively develop toward their common ideal. This is the relationship between the Heaven, Earth, and man. Take a small family as an example. If the husband and the wife, the father and the son, the brothers and the sisters can live and work together with one heart, make their efforts together, love each other dearly, then it must be a harmonious and happy family.

The condition of man and all things is like this. In the microcosmic material world, any molecule of matter is combined in order by atom and electron. Here, "in order" refers to the harmony of coexistence. Once the harmony is destroyed, disturbance and struggle will be brought about, even altering the features of the matter would.

The condition of both small and large things are like this. Therefore, no matter what things mankind is going to alter, the "order" (inner relationship and the rules) should be understood first, thus guiding them in accord with the rule. Only by thus doing, can mankind get twice the result with half the effort. Otherwise, things will go contrary to the original wish.

Through careful observation and practice from various things of the Heaven, Earth, and man, I hold that the essential relationships between man and man, man and thing, thing and thing, in the world and in the Universe, are coexisting while opposing one another; they are tolerant then stable; they are harmonious then resonant. This is, after all, the highest natural dialectics and the fundamental law of the Universe.

We now clearly understand the positive significance embodied in the old legend of Pan Gu's opening of the Heaven and the Earth. First, this legend reflects the fundamental law of the Universe. Second, in order not to let down the great task entrusted by the Chaos, Pan Gu devoted himself to the cause of creating things and breeding man. Such a noble spirit is held in high esteem!

The word "spirit" is apt to bring many associations in the minds of the people who are vivid in thought. If the two Chinese characters *jin shen* (meaning spirit) are divided and the latter is studied, one will feel even more puzzled. There are three explanations found in common Chinese dictionaries as to the character *shen:* 1) It is called by the superstitious believers as the creator of the Heaven, Earth, and all things, as well as the demon or spirit of the deceased, who are their worship of idols. (This explanation has still two other meanings: a) extraordinary, extremely super excellent; b) unbelievable, most curious.) 2) Mental vigor, thinking ability, attention. 3) Air, expression.

 We will not evaluate for the time being if these explanations are suitable and encompassing or not, yet to think and study them will make the word *shen* even more confusing to us. With the exception of the "expression" explained in the third item, which is slightly concrete, the rest of the explanations are invisible and untouchable and are hard to describe and express with accurate and precise words. Thus, they are unable to be set in a range and standard with a precise yardstick. What measure can we utilize to confirm their existence or not?

From the objective view point, there really are many things in the world that are invisible and untouchable to human beings. Take the body of everyone. There is spirit, thought (or thinking ability), and vitality. These are all invisible and untouchable, yet undeniable. The most outstanding characteristic of these things is that they all exist opposite of material things and have their subjective initiative. Therefore, terms such as "spirit and matter," "soul and flesh," are often spoken.

Modern scientific knowledge also tells us that combining two or more matter substances may compound a new matter. But no spirit can be composed, nor can they compound vitality! It is obvious, then, that "spirit and matter," "soul and flesh" are really two things with different properties. The knowledge of modern medical science also enables us to understand that when a man dies naturally (without suffering from any disease), the matters that constructs his body are found without any loss—only his vitality is exhausted and can no longer govern the material substances in his body to carry on the metabolism—thus he passes away. We can see that though vitality attaches itself to matter, matter is by no means equal to vitality.

Now a question is put solemnly. Aside from the three elements of time, space, and matter in the Universe, there is still another element: spirit. Spirit is what we might as well generally call those kinds of things that belong neither to time and space nor to the material realm.

The fundamental meaning of spirit refers to the initiative ability that surpasses the material realm. Time, space, matter, and spirit are the four great elements of the Universe— the composition of which amplify myriads of things. If the composition is good, the derivatives will be more stable and long lasting; if not, they will be turbulent, unresting, and meet a premature end. Such a condition can also be found in our body. The degree of good or bad composition of spirit and matter, of flesh and soul will directly influence the result of the deriving things. These kinds of compositions certainly run through the relationship of "existing while opposing, being tolerant then stable, being harmonious then resonant," so as to measure their good and bad and make the choice of whether to accept or to reject!

The natural law which we are familiar with has an item that goes: "the survival of the fittest, the elimination of the unfit." But what is fit? Fit means "suit" or "adapt." That is, to accommodate mutually, and not to harm each other, but to complement each other. Then everything can live peacefully and be everlasting! Is not the fine circulation in the natural world a good explanation on this question?

Any man with normal physiological functions may not deny that man is provided with vitality and thinking ability. Having obtained this basic cognition, we can carry on a detailed and reasonable corollary on the question of "the Spirit existing in the Universe," which seems rather fantastic.

Man is subordinate to the mother body: the Earth. Does the Earth that possesses man, then, permit the thinking ability and vitality of men to exist like their bodies? The answer is affirmative since they are in fact already existing! In other words, in the general conception of all things that are contained in the Earth, there exists the spirit (the vitality and the thinking ability as well as all initiative capacities that surpass material features). We may briefly say, then, that there exists spirit on Earth.

The Earth is subordinate to the Universe, and is an element of the Universe. People are sure to believe this point of view, because it is also a fact which can not be denied. Thus, a conclusion may be drawn that now that the Earth, which is subordinate to the Universe, possesses spirit, the Universe that contains the Earth certainly possesses spirit! Since the Universe is boundless, the spirit existing on the Earth cannot fly out from the Universe to look for a place to exist there. We may briefly say, then, that there is spirit in the Universe.

Anybody who is mentally sound and is ready to cognize the Universe objectively will not again deny the fact of the existence of spirit in the Universe. The confirmation of the existence of spirit in the Universe is tantamount to the cognizing of mankind the existence of matter in the Universe. This will certainly bring a qualitative leap in cognizing the actual state of the Universe so as to carry on self-remolding and to reform the nature with the ever more appropriate and all-round knowledge, as well as to bring happiness to mankind and to ourselves more effectively.

The existence of matter in the Universe is by no means limited to the Earth; the existence of matter on Earth is only a miniature of the existence of matter in the Universe. The form of the existence of matter on Earth is only some expression of the existence of matter in the Universe. They have their general character (universality) and their individual character (particularity).

The outstanding universality of the existence of matter lies in the following two elements: 1) The law of conservation of matter. The material elements in the Earth are conservative and also in the Universe; 2) The existence in order. For instance, the Earth has its own set, revolving orbit, as do other celestial bodies. The orderly arrangement of the atoms and molecules inside matter is not by any means monopolized by the Earth.

Could the existence of spirit in the Universe come into being relative to the features of the existence of matter? Considering the homologous relationship between the various things and matter in the world, a bold supposition may be put forward.

The existence of spirit in the Universe, like the existence of matter, is by no means confined only to the Earth. It has also the feature of conservation, the characteristic of order, even a stronger, tighter, and more rigorous orderly feature—for it possesses subjective initiative capacity that surpasses matter. If this supposition is tenable, all enigmas in the Universe will be easily solved, and we can make a reasonable and overall deduction to the true feature and essence of the Universe and the origin and development of a myriad of things.

The real feature of the Universe is this: the Universe is a boundless thing, without a beginning or an end; the four elements of time, space, matter, and spirit constitute a whole body of the Universe. The general body of the respective four elements possesses infinite characteristics, so they cannot be measured as to their number and length.

The universality and the individuality of the four elements

in the Universe are all passive; spirit is active. Time, space, and spirit are invisible, yet matter is visible. Therefore, time, space, and spirit seem visionary and indiscernible, yet matter looks real and true. In the commonly constituted mother body, they are mutually dependent on each other and are combinable and divisible. Division refers to the mother body and among others respectively, but no matter how they divide they are unable to be divisible so far as to be rid of the mother body. They are determined by the outstanding feature of the mother body: boundless and without beginning or end. Therefore, their overall composition is eternal.

Time and space cannot fluctuate matter and matter but are able to offer infinitely spacious stage and time for the transformation and fluctuation of matter and matter. In the family of material elements (particles), they may gather together or they may scatter. When they are perfectly scattered, they will dissociate and wander in space; when they gather, new matter will be produced (better to say material substance). Spirit possesses a characteristic corresponding to matter and may also gather or scatter in the family of its own body. Yet, its expression is invisible (as is man's thought), but once it takes part in matter's gathering and scattering (it may also be called on to carry on transformation in the combination with matter), the transformation and fluctuation of matter and thing will be more fantastic, strange, and more orderly (rational and planned).

The fundamental relationship between the four elements, especially the relationship between spirit and matter, are all co-existing while also in opposition, being tolerant than stable, being harmonious then resonant.

Since the Universe possesses such a natural character and the four great elements constituting the Universe are provided with these characteristics and relationship, we men and things of today that were bred, unavoidably maintain and reflect more or less their features and relations.

Another question should now be emphasized, namely: What kind of material substance (matter) and man will be bred by the composition of the four essential elements in the Universe to fit best with their fundamental features and basic relation? In other words, they need a process of selection.

Through comparison and selection, a best scheme can be adopted and put into effect. The human and material world which were created at last by putting into effect such kinds of schemes will definitely be eternal. After all, eternity is the sublime form of expression of their universality and individuality.

Did Pan Gu Really Exist?

Analyzing the view of "spirit existing in the Universe," the answer is affirmative: Pan Gu did in fact exist. Moreover, the form of Pan Gu's existence is none other than the following possibilities: 1) he is the sublime representative of the spirit in the Universe; 2) he is the sublime representative of spirit and material substance in the Universe; and 3) he is the sublime representative bred together by the four essential elements of the Universe. Provided that Pan Gu was not provided with one of the three possibilities, he would be unqualified to represent the Universe to open up the Heaven and the Earth, to create things, and to breed man.

By analyzing the essential elements (matter and thing) of the Earth and the Universe above, we can definitely draw the following supposition: Pan Gu is the sublime spirit, possessing greatest reason and might. He was bold enough to accept the mission from the Chaos (or the ideal set by himself), to reform the turbulent (disorder) Chaos into a methodical (orderly) Universe, and finally to create a harmonious and fine eternal world. He then carried on the great practice, devoted his body heroically to create things and breed man, so as to get beneficial experience and to realize the great ideal afterward.

Since Pan Gu is the sublime spirit and because both spirit and matter possess the feature of conservation, although Pan Gu devoted his body (yet did not really die), his spirit still exists. The spirit of Pan Gu kept instructing his flesh and blood body to mingle into the Universal matter and to compose itself with them, to make experiments and practices of creating things and breeding man and to keep making summaries. He knew that in order to create a fine eternal world, one should exert his utmost. Pan Gu earnestly hoped that the mankind bred by him could be admitted into the fine future. As such, he created a complex and agonizing world to temper the people, to enable them to qualify to enter the eternity. In order to guide the people when they are in agony and in perplexity, and to refrain them from going astray-as seen in the different periods of the history-Pan Gu used many ways to make people understand reason, to guide them to do good, to enable them to march forward to the peaceful and fine direction through exerting their utmost.

Does it suddenly dawn upon us now the reason why our ancestors compiled the story dealing with "Pan Gu opening the Heaven and the Earth," and the positive and instructive significance it represents? Otherwise, how could our ancestors compile the natural dialectics with so abstruse and recondite various corresponding relations?

Having attained this profound understanding, we can cognize correctly the real value, meaning, and direction of our own existence.

As for myself, it was because I had made repeated observations, experiences, pondering, and summaries on the above theory and things regarding to the Heaven, Earth, and man, and because I had obtained after some curious and anguishing experiences over a ten year period some skill and technique of curing sickness, I profoundly realized that I should devote my knowledge and skill to relieve more people from agony, to bring happiness to others and to myself at the same time. Thus, I originated the Pan Gu Mystical Qigong.

The Truth of Pan Gu Mystical Qigong

We can simplify the above theory and philosophy with the following definitions and explanations.

Pan Gu Mystical Qigong was founded according to the dialectical relations of various material substances and things embodied in the formation, the development, and the trend of Heaven, Earth, and man. Therefore, the mode of the *gong* (exercise) condenses highly the advantageous factors for man and things in the Universe, and it is provided with certain automatic adjustable functions. So long as the people who exercise this qigong form are willing to conduct themselves properly in society and to demand themselves according to the principle of behaving, and the key philosophy of "taking kindness and benevolence as its basis, taking frankness and friendliness as its bosom," they can obtain the skills of curing disease, strengthening body, developing knowledge, and being peaceful and harmonious. After having indulged themselves in exercising the qigong movements and closely integrating this practice with the theory in the wonderful book, *The Path of Life*, the practitioners will reach a splendid realm of the Universe and man being two in one. In other words, the spirit and flesh highly unite and strike a sympathetic chord with the conservation of the Universe, then transit to the eternal human world.

If it is described with concrete characters, it can be comprehended in the other name of this qigong form, *Qian Kun Qigong* (The Sun and Moon Qigong).

Qian Kun, or the sun and the moon, are none other than the Heaven, the Earth, the Sun, and the Moon. By common sense, nobody can deny that our present human beings (indeed, all living things) are living in the mutual opposition and mutual balance of the Heaven and the Earth, the Sun and the Moon. If ever the perfect relation between the four elements lost balance, the existence of mankind will be directly influenced, and possibly even destroyed. This, if even one of the four elements is missing!

The material elements that bear and breed us are from the Heaven and the Earth, the energy that can influence directly our physique mainly comes from the sun and the moon. We are living in such a time and space environment where everything we are facing has never received influence from the sun and moon directly or indirectly. Therefore, we can only conform to them and from them absorb nourishment, energy, and philosophic theories that are beneficial to us, so as to better exist. The saying that "those who submit to the Heaven will prosper, those who resist the Heaven shall perish," tells the very argument of it.

In the mode of the *gong* or exercise of Pan Gu Mystical Qigong, I take "Absorbing the cream of the sun and the moon and the vital energy from the Heaven and the Earth to strengthen body and health, to suppress the evils and publicize the merits, to relieve the mankind and to lead the people," as the purpose of practicing qigong exercises. I also advocate "Taking kindliness and benevolence as its basis, taking frankness and friendliness as its bosom," as the principle and key to the mode of the exercise practice. Here's why:

It is just under the consideration of these reasons that I deem the mode of this qigong form should be simple to practice and easy to learn; its idea, intention, and will must be implicit, reserved; time required must be short and the effect should be quick. Only by meeting these requirements can it be in keeping with man's life, and tally with the various mysterious, wonderful relations among the Heaven, Earth, and man. It is a way of simplifying by cutting out the superfluities, returning to the simplicity, and reverting to the truth. Of course, it can only be performed by putting into effect the principle of "turning mystery into reality, turning complexity into simplicity." One must accumulate the various factors that are beneficial to man in the Universe and to turn them into invisible information which is poured into the mode of the gong exercise and represented by simple motions and intention. So long as the practitioners read silently the key of the qigong practice (to open the door of receiving the information) and practicing the exercises, they can receive continually the information which will produce dynamic and positive effects in the human body.

This kind of effect manifests itself mainly in two aspects: 1) it enables the practitioners to absorb directly the material elements from the great nature so as to cure the diseases caused by the lack of or by the superfluity of such material elements. For the people who do not fall sick, it will enable the material elements to maintain balance in their body and make their body more healthy; and 2) it strengthens the physiological functions of the various organs in the body, so as to regain and maintain exuberant vitality.

The above is the content and the knowledge of the exercise of the Pan Gu Mystical Qigong.

The statement I would like to put forth here is: Anything in the world, even the best one, when it is put to use by man, is only an objective factor. If we want it to give the rein to better effect, one should exert subjective efforts to coordinate or compose with it. Thus, we must solve the question of whether good coordination or good composition can be obtained. Therefore, different effects will definitely be produced, which is a normal phenomenon. So is the Pan Gu Mystical Qigong. The effect available in someone may be quicker and greater, but in others may be slower and smaller. But only by firmly reminding yourself of the principle of "absorbing the *qi* to nourish the body, tempering the mind to cultivate the root," and persisting in exercising the gong, can we reap a good effect.

4

Characteristics of Pan Gu Mystical Qigong

What is Qigong?

Since the making of mankind's history, especially in China, people have continuously been studying the question of what qigong truly is.

The records found in many ancient Chinese books, such as Emperor Huang's *Nei Jing* (Internal Classics) and *Yi Jin Jing* (The Book of Changes), have revealed the orbit and the yield in the research of our ancestors, in addition to many daily used idioms and phrases. In describing the vigor of life, attributive phrases such as "the flourishing *qi* in the morning," "the vital qi of the youngster," "the *qi* appearing like rainbows," and in describing the declining of life as "the seriously hurt *qi*," and "the faintly remained *qi*," often meet our eyes. Actually, the word *qi* in such phrases very much concretely expresses and describes the original or basic vitality of human life. However, many people use these phrases often, but neglect their real meaning. If they didn't, the mysteries which artificially cover qigong would be thinner and lack in density.

The understanding and study of the qigong of our ancestors is in fact full of plain materialism, emphasizing practice even more than esteeming perceptual knowledge. For instance, the expressions of light, image, figure, shadow, and idea are all experienced during qigong practice; and the feelings of bloatedness, numbness, coldness, heat, and pain are also a real reflection of proper practice. The above is the recognition of materialsim or, you may say, the recognitions which are obtained through the means of materialism. Moreover, our ancestors divided the knowledge of *qi* in detail and concluded in proper description. For the large one there is the *qi* of Chaos: "*Qi* of light and blue floated upward forming the Heaven, and the heavy *qi* centered downward forming the Earth." For the small one there is the "vitality *qi*" in the human body and the "spirit *qi*" of all things in Earth (i.e., the *qi* in qigong). The above shows the broad and narrow meaning of *qi*; the former one is the broadest, while the *qi* in qigong is comparatively the narrower one. Thus, our ancestors used the word *qi* to show its characteristic.

The broad meaning of *qi* specializes the general characteristic, while the narrow meaning specializes the definite characteristic. Therefore, the broad meaning embodies the narrow meaning and the latter expresses some characteristics (general characteristic) of the former—such are the things in the world. For example, the conception of man is also divided into broad and narrow meanings. This is the individual man, a group of people, and human beings in general. There are differences in general between general characteristics and definite characteristics—both are mingled together but at the same time different.

The *qi* in qigong, which is from the *qi* in Universe, is of the most spiritual kind, thus a special way (i.e., qigong exercise) is required to obtain it.

What is the Qi in the Universe?

Our ancestors derived at a clear understanding of the phrase: "*Qi* of light and blue one floated upward forming the Heaven and the heavy qi centered and sank downward forming the Earth." Here, *qi* is virtually the tiny particles of matter in the Universe. Its own law of motion describing qi is as follows: "Light and blue things float upward, forming clear and infinite sky (as such, the Chinese character meaning "sky" was written as "blue air"); heavy and turbid things sank and formed the ground (the Earth, the stars, and nebula). This, in fact, not only is the recognition of the motion of matter during the Chaos but also the interpretation of the phenomenon of matter motion after space formed. Such a phenomenon even now is often perceivable—quantities of particles are found floating here and there in the sky. While only the light and blue particles can keep floating in the air, heavy and turbid things are doomed to eventually sink to the ground. This is the characteristic in the broadest sense of "original *qi*."

With the above mentioned points in mind, we now hold that the real source of the *qi* in qigong can be understood and realized. It is from the Universe and is a special thing, having both material and spiritual characteristics.

The *qi* in qigong shows its material characteristics in three ways:

1) It reveals its existence through energy. So when *qi* is touched by the body of man, certain corresponding feelings such as bloatedness, numbness, coldness, pain, itching, unconscious swing, and a stream of air running in the body can be detected.

The same reasoning can be applied to it when the other energies (e.g., electric energy, thermal energy) are touched by the human body and a feeling is detected. The difference lies in the fact that instruments have been made to detect the existence of electric and other energies, while no suitable instrument has yet been made to detect the existence of *qi*. Thus, it seems as if there are no scientific proof as to the existence of *qi*.

One of my students, a retired worker of the Guangdong Base Engineering Company, often detects a feeling of electric strokes and finds electric sparkles appearing between his hands when he is receiving *qi* and exercising qigong as prescribed in this book. When issuing *qi* to treat patients of the opposite sex, the electric strokes are felt in both sides and electric sparkles can also be perceived. This phenomenon shows that it emphasizes the ways shown in his body through the measure of electric energy.

As the *qi* field (or biological field) differs in everybody, each obtain a different feeling when touching *qi* (i.e., some feel electric energy more while others feel light energy or magnetic energy more).

2) *Qi* moves in and across time and space in the way of molecular motion.

In daily life, we can often smell the fragrance of flowers, the pleasant odors of food, and other scents. This is because the nose of man absorbs the molecules of matter or material substances coming from near places. One can accept this reasoning even with a little knowledge of physics.

Along the same lines, odors are smelled by the practitioner of qigong while in the *gong* state (the state of *gong*-receiving or *gong*-exercising).

After having realized its hows and whys, we can understand that the process of exercising and receiving *qi* is practically the same process as receiving the energy and absorbing the material elements from nature.

Moreover, a foul, dead body odor will be smelt when the patient suffering from organic disease inflammation (e.g., when a certain organ is deteriorated and decayed) is being treated by the one who acquires a profound and consummate qigong skill. It is well explained that the issuing *qi* dissolved the deteriorated parts inside the organ in the body into tiny particles as small as molecules, and discharged and ejected them out of the body. Thus, the people around the patient will smell such bad odors, and its material characteristic is then obvious.

3) It launches outward in the mode of a "field." Like an electric field or a magnetic field, while a *qi* field is launching outward, it also forms circles by circles, as waves urge waves. It is out of the question for a man with strong issuing ability to launch the *qi* far—say, hundreds or thousands of miles.

Long Distance Healing

July, 1991 witnessed my primitive curing of one of my patients over a long distance. One evening, Mr. Ji Xiao Ming, an overseas Chinese who had made my acquaintance in 1991 during his stay in China and was then living in the Dominican Republic, phoned me from the official residence of the secretary-general of the president of the country. He asked me to issue long distance qigong to cure his friend's mother (the secretary-general's mother), who was suffering from chronic nephritis, and the sister, who was suffering from a migraine. I agreed to offer them an experimental issuing. The interpreter translated the method of receiving *qi* instructed by me, then we hung up the receiver. I began to issue *qi* in Sheng Zheng; they were receiving *qi* in Dominica. After fifteen minutes, they called me again and were glad to inform me that they both had detected the feeling and the secretary-general's sister found her headache disappeared and suffered no more!

A number of my students have acquired the ability to issue long distance *qi* and have produced fairly good curative effects. Of which, two had cooperated with each other in Guangzhou to give first-aid treatment with the skill of long distance perspective and long distance issuing *qi* to cure a patient in critical condition in Foshan, who was suffering from a cardiovascular disease.

It seems fantastic and unbelievable for those who have not experienced such things in person to believe the curative effects of *qi* through long distances. What is more, no proper scientific instrument is available to detect the process in creating the effect. As such, it becomes more unconvincable. But the cured patients are the best witnesses and whose testimony is convincing.

As another example, Ms. Liang Wei, the head of the Personnel Department of Guangzhou University, suffered from cholecystitis on May 11, 1994, owing to over work, and was soaked through with a cold sweat caused by a cutting pain. As a rule, she had to be hospitalized for several days. However, at that time she was attending a meeting in ChongHua, so it was inconvenient for her to stay in the hospital. Fortunately, she had some knowledge regarding to the receiving of *qi* from a distance for curing diseases. Therefore, she called and asked me to issue *qi* to cure her. Only a short time after she had received *qi* she felt that the pain begin to ease, and she fell asleep the very evening. The next morning she went to work as usual. The fact that not even a tablet of medicine was needed, and long distance *qi* treatment resulted in such wonderful curative effect, made the people who saw and learned of it in person feel strange, but they had to realize the truth. They then were determined to learn Pan Gu Mystical Qigong.

Explaining the Phenomenon

In my opinion, this phenomenon can be compared with the launching and receiving principle in radio, for it is a special "field" in objective reality. If only you know how to receive *qi* with the corresponding specific means, you can receive *qi* to obtain its curing effect. Having learned the material characteristic of qigong, we may say that we have understood half of the principle of the question on why qigong can be used for disease treatment. And this partial understanding can be traced to the same origin as medical principles (including Western and traditional Chinese medicine).

What is the principle of modern medical science? The most fundamental principle is to suit the remedy to the case. Concretely speaking, the medicine is used to replenish the need of the organs in the body so as to solve the factors causing the illness.

Why does man contract disease? There are only two basic reasons for this:

1) The organs in the human body either lack the necessary matter elements or the harmful matter elements increase, thus contracting a disease. Diseases are mostly classified into parenchymal diseases and can be examined easily. We call them diseases of material characteristics.

2) Various physiologic functions within the human body work continuously. However, once some decline or troubles appear in such functions, the human body would also contract the diseases.

At the beginning, even in a period of time, the ailments of this kind have not yet shown themselves as organic diseases, but they make the patients feel easily tired and fatigued. Though general malaise and aches are felt here and there, pathogen and ailments can hardly be checked out. Thus, we classify such symptoms into diseases with spiritual characteristics. However, once such kind of ailments have turned into parenchyma ones, they will be serious or chronic and difficult to cure. They include, for example, cardiopathy, diabetes mellitus, cerebral embolism, psychosis, chronic hepatitis, lupus erythematosus, and rheumatoid arthritis.

Modern medical science has satisfactorily solved the ailments evoked by the causes of the first group. Yet, in curing the ailments evoked by the cause of the second group, or together with the cause of the first group, it shows itself incapable and the curative effects are often found unsatisfactory.

Let us now explore the reason why such phenomenon exist. The basic principle of modern medical science (especially Western medical science) is based on matter characteristic: to replenish matter with matter (i.e., to replenish material elements that the body needs and to neutralize the harmful material elements in the body with medicine); or to rid matter with matter (i.e., to incise the infected part or organ). However, it lacks an effective means to fundamentally strengthen the vitality (physiologic function) and immune systems in the human body.

The characteristics of qigong agree with the characteristics of spiritual motion in vitality. Therefore, it is the other half of the explanation of why qigong is able to cure disease: qigong is able to solve the second kind of causes for contracting diseases in the human body.

Let us now move on to a discussion of the word spirit. However, when discussing the word spirit, the definition of spirit should first be exactly and correctly appreciated.

What is spirit? The main meaning of spirit is the dynamic ability that surpasses matter characteristics. Let's take the vitality of human beings as an example. Humans possess a dynamic ability that surpasses matter characteristics. Though the vitality adheres to matter (e.g., the human body) and acts on matter (e.g., the human body), matter is by no means equal to vitality! Thus, the phenomena "decease coming upon the man without any ailment" is the best testimony. Should matter be equal to vitality, the quantity of matter that forms various organs in the human body would not decrease. And, what is more, should all organs in the body contract no disease, then the vitality would continue to exist. However, facts prove to the contrary. Vitality exists (e.g., is a "thing") without any trace, form, sign, mark, or even a shadow. Nevertheless, once it ceases to work, decease will come upon man; and once it is unable to effectively make certain organs work properly, the body will fall ill.

The dynamic ability of vitality shows itself in two aspects: action of consciousness and action of super consciousness. At a certain degree, it acts on the will of man. So, strong-willed and/or open-minded people can persist longer and recover quicker when they are contracted with diseases than those who are of weaker will and mind. This is the expression of vitality in conscious action.

In most cases, however, it obeys not the will of the body but acts voluntarily on its own mode to work actively or slow down until it prostrates itself of its own accord. This action of super consciousness of vitality will produce both favorable or unfavorable effects on the health of the human body. When it is in its vigorous and exuberant state, as in youth, it creates good effect. As such, slight wounds or minor ailments can be quickly recovered without the need of ingesting medicine, but only by the automatically adjusted affect of its own vitality. If man's vitality can remain in a vigorous and energetic state, and in an automatically adjusted condition, then there are hopeful prospects and outlooks in maintaining real health in the human body.

Coincidentally, the *qi* in qigong possesses conscious action and super conscious action, thus agreeing with the characteristic of vitality. The active characteristic of human vitality, through proper qigong exercising, can therefore be strengthened. In other words, the physiologic functions of the body are strengthened and unimaginable effects are accordingly obtained in treating some diseases. (Certainly, this result of strengthening physiologic functions may vary in the messages contained in different measures of qigong. Therefore, no sectarian measures of qigong can completely strengthen various physiologic functions in the human body, thus resulting in the appearance that some diseases cannot be cured by certain qigong exercises.)

While I am unable to offer data to explain the process of why *qi* can strengthen man's physiologic functions, I can provide a large number of facts to testify as to the successful effects of *qi* and qigong.

Healing Effects of Pan Gu Mystical Qigong

Pan Gu Mystical Qigong has produced wonderful effects in treating cardiopathy. As a point of fact, every patient who came to me with heart disease and who has learned and properly practiced the qigong exercises obtained positive results. Among them, some have completely recovered. One of my patients, who suffered from an intermittent heart beat caused by a heart deformation, once suffered a ten minute period with no heart beat! He was rescued after receiving the treatment of Pan Gu Mystical Qigong. After six months of treatments from me and his own self-practice, a hospital diagnosis showed that his deformed heart grew unexpectedly and was normal again!

In treating other diseases of disorder in physiologic function and immunity decline, this qigong form has also produced miraculous effects. For example, Mr. Fang Ling, a retired teacher of Guangzhou Foreign Trade Institute, found senile scars appearing on his arms several years ago. However, after several months of exercising this qigong form they disappeared and his skin feels smooth again. This phenomenon sufficiently proves that the practice of Pan Gu Mystical Qigong strengthened the physiologic function of his skin.

The most typical case of strengthening the human immune system is when a group of patients suffering from lupus erythematosus and rheumatoid arthritis recovered after being treated with this qigong form. Take Ms. Ye Ping, for example. She is a teacher of No. 97 Middle School in Guangzhou. In July, 1992, she was diagnosed to have contracted lupus erythematosus. The doctor emphatically told her that the cause of such an ailment could not yet be determined, and that it was firmly believed to be beyond remedy. However, to control the condition, she was to take medicine (hormones) at definite times and doses throughout the remainder of her life. Fortunately, on the recommendation of her friend, Ms. Ping began to learn Pan Gu Mystical Qigong in December of 1992. Her condition improved. After a subsequent check-up on December 27, 1993, the result showed that data indicate normalcy, the lines on two lungs became comparatively normal, there are no infiltrated lesion seen in the lungs, and abnormalities are no longer seen in the heart.

The above examples have led me to realize the matter and spiritual characteristic of Pan Gu Mystical Qigong, and to have an overall realization of it, so as to better grasp the specialty of qigong and to cure the patients with better effect.

I wish that all people in the world are in good health! I wish that all people in the world are friendly and kind! I hold: For realizing my best wishes, the miraculous but real qigong will bring a new hope and a feasible and practical thoroughfare.

5

The Spectrum of Pan Gu Mystical Qigong

The following is an abridged transcription of a speech I gave at the inaugural meeting of the Guangzhou Pan Gu Mystical Qigong Research Association.

Leaders, guests, and fellow students: I am deeply obliged to you this evening for your joining the inaugural meeting of Guangzhou Pan Gu Mystical Qigong Research Association and would like to wish you a good health, a happy family, and a pleasant life on this occasion. I also take this opportunity to express my sincere appreciation of the presence and the guidance of the leaders concerned from the provincial and municipal Qigong Scientific Research Institutes, from the Guangzhou Municipal General Union of Physical Culture, from Guangzhou Municipal Civil Administration, and from Guangzhou University.

Now let me give you a briefing to the Pan Gu Mystical Qigong.

Pan Gu Mystical Qigong is a special knowledge with matter and spiritual characteristics. I personally hold that the material characteristic of qigong shows itself in three ways: 1) as a specific energy, 2) as the special mode of molecular motion, and 3) as a kind of field.

What is the spiritual characteristic of qigong? My explanation to this is that the initiative capacity that surpasses material characteristics is spirit. It seems that man's vitality, man's thinking capacity are hard to explain by the material characteristics which are familiar to us. Our vitality and thinking capacity are not visible. Be this as it may, invisibility is on no account proof of their nonexistence.

I classify all things that are provided with initiative ability, but are temporarily hard to explain, with the material characteristic into spirit. Qigong possesses initiative ability. When talking about qigong's material and spiritual characteristics, especially it being a form of energy, I would like to spend two or three minutes to make an experiment.

Here I take a visible way to issue *qi* to all of you and let's see if you feel it or not, because I advocate practicing and experimenting. Now, please follow my example in maneuvering your hands: put your right hand above the left hand of your right neighbor without touching it, with a distance of ten to fifteen centimeters, keep motionless, then see what your feeling is. Very well, sit down please.

The philosophical view of Pan Gu Mystical Qigong is the harmony among the Heaven, Earth, and man. I personally deem that in the world and in the Universe, all the relationships—including between man and man, between man and things, between things and things—coexisting while opposing, are tolerant then stable, are harmonious then resonant.

The how and why of Pan Gu Mystical Qigong is to decide its contents according to the knowledge that life originated from the Universe, to the physiological construction of the human body, and to the relationship between man and great nature. We know from the knowledge of science that any living things have a close relationship with the energy of the sun, the moon, and even the Universe. In fact, and as an example, the growth of everything depends upon the sun. The photosynthesis of any plant can only be carried out under the sun, thus the plant, absorbs more effectively the useful material elements from the soil and the air, so as to expand, strengthen, and keep itself alive. Indeed, other animals, including humans, also need sunlight to survive. If a man is out of the touch of sun light for a year, he would find himself inferior in his constitutions. The sun-energy brings to the human body both good and bad effects at the same time. According to all these relations and their features, the mode of Pan Gu Mystical Qigong is to absorb mainly the elements from the sun, the moon, and the Universe which are beneficial to human body, while rejecting their harmful elements.

The tenets of curing diseases of Pan Gu Mystical Qigong shows itself in two aspects: firstly, through exercising the *gong*, to absorb the matter elements that are useful to the human body directly from the great nature, so as to cure the diseases caused by the lack of the material elements or the superfluity of the harmful matter elements in man's organs. Secondly, through exercising the *gong*, to strengthen man's physiological function, and to cure the diseases caused by the obstruction of the physiological function in the organs of the human body.

As a result of its possessing such contents and the above medical tenet, Pan Gu Mystical Qigong's curing effect and realm are comparatively effective and wide-based. I have given treatments for many kinds of diseases–with the exception of aids–and have garnered successful results. This qigong form especially brings extraordinary effect to illnesses due to heart disease and immunity.

Without exception, those who suffer from heart disease but persist in exercising the qigong have acquired a positive healing effect. Its treatment in the diseases due to the obstruction of immunity, such as lupus erythematosus, has brought many positive examples as to its true healing ability. In point of fact, many patients have thoroughly recovered or taken a turn for the better through exercising Pan Gu Mystical Qigong.

Take, for example, my classmate Ye Ping, who suffered from lupus erythematosus. After exercising Pan Gu Mystical Qigong for a period of time, she has fully recovered. Moreover, our classmate Liu Rong Hua, who suffered from rheumatoid arthritis for eighteen years, has now come around completely.

Lupus erythematosus and the like are diseases caused by the obstruction of the immune system, and are difficult to cure by modern medical science. Why? I personally deem that modern medical science puts emphasis mainly on material characteristics in studying and treating disease. Thus, in treating the diseases, due to the superfluity of the harmful elements or the lack of necessary material elements in the human body, they get outstanding effects by taking medicine that neutralizes and to replenishes them. However, the diseases caused by immunity, along with other chronic diseases whose main etiologic cause is due to the fatigue and the wear of the physiological organs and functions after continuous work, lead to the formation of the obstruction of physiological functions. Serious physiological function obstruction will then produce disease. No very effective method can be found in modern medical science to cure physiological function senescence. The exception is the practice mode of Pan Gu Mystical Qigong.

I took this important cause of falling ill (e.g., the wear and obstruction of physiological function) into consideration. I added this information into it and comparatively curative effects were brought in curing this kind of disease. Many patients not only recovered from their illness after exercising the *gong* but looked younger than before.

Take Mr. Fang Ning as a typical example. He is an old intellectual who has been researching qigong for over thirty years and has learned many schools of practicing the mode of qigong. However, he finally agreed to practice my set of qigong exercises. Why? Because he agreed with my theory of qigong and then experienced a transformation in his body after practice. He is now seventy-one years old and in good health. A few years ago, there appeared senile plaque on his hands, and his skin turned out to be quite wrinkled.

Again, however, after exercising my set of qigong exercises for several months, the senile plaque disappeared and his skin became smoother.

Thus, this gives eloquent proof of the possibility of the enhancing and recovering of the body's physiological function through the practice of these qigong exercises? Since the mode of Pan Gu Mystical Qigong is free from any school's conception, it does not follow the belief that "It will only work only if you believe it will or only if you are sincere."

In essence, Pan Gu Mystical Qigong advocates the way of "Taking practice as the teacher, taking society as the master." That is to say, we should take practice as our master, our best teacher. To testify and to carry forward it through practice is what I hope. And I further wish that after the founding of the Pan Gu Mystical Qigong Research Association our schoolmates might continually study, research, and develop it so as to cure more patients and to bring happiness to mankind with better a Spirit of practice.

6

The Range of Disease Cure of Pan Gu Mystical Qigong

Pan Gu Mystical Qigong may bring curative effects to various kinds of diseases without contraindication. Eleven categories of diseases curable through the practice of the exercises detailed in this book are listed below.

1) Palpitation, coronary heart disease, hypertension, hypoglycemia, and intracranial hypertension

2) Neurogenic headache, migraine headache, laryngopharynx ache, shoulder ache, abdomen ache, and pain from wounded extremities

3) Insomnia and neurasthenia

4) Retinitis, allergic rhinitis, tracheitis, cervical spine infection, ankylosis of spinaitis, hepatitis, and nephritis

5) Stomach disease, dysfunction of gastro-intestinal tract, duodenal ulcer, diarrhea, constipation, and hemorrhoids

6) Cold and fever

7) Vertigo and motion sickness

8) Thyroid adenoma, benign fibroma, malignant lymphoma, cancer of cavum, and cancer of liver

9) Rheumatic arthritis and rheumatoid

10) Cataract, hyperthyroidism, tuberculosis of the lymphatic gland, asthma, endocrine disorder, spur, cholelithiasis, hepatic cirrhosis, and diabetes mellitus

11) Dull distention in chest and vexation, mental worry and distress, pessimismand disappointment, irascible and angry dispositions

While Pan Gu Mystical Qigong is capable of curing all kinds of diseases, it in no way claims to be 100 percent effective in all cases. Proper and complete curing depends mainly on the subjective efforts of the practitioner and on their comprehension of the mode (exercises), the tenets of the *gong*, and on their understanding and effort toward the training and hard tempering of Spirit and flesh.

7

Questions and Answers

What gong (exercise) modes are included in Pan Gu Mystical Qigong?

Pan Gu Mystical Qigong contains a complete set of exercises, and consists of moving *gong* and static *gong* dialectically, in which the former one is the basis. It is, however, more effective when the two are combined.

Who will be qualified to exercise static qigong?

Firstly, those who have exercised moving *gong* for more than two months. Secondly, those who have gained some effects from their exercising. Thirdly, those who are willing to probe the secrets of the Universe and the life and to further study and discuss the book *The Path of Life*.

What is the benefit of joining the heightening class?

"Practice is the basis, comprehension is a short-cut." The subjects of the class are given special lectures on *The Path of Life*, the mode and the tenet of Pan Gu Mystical Qigong given by Master Ou, which aims at heightening the theoretical level and the power of qigong. Therefore, those who have learned the qigong for one month should try to join the heightening class.

Is there any influence in the other mode of qigong an exerciser may have previously learned prior to Pan Gu Mystical Qigong?

Pan Gu Mystical Qigong is free from any taboo and commandment, any conception of faction and school. So long as the exercisers get the key of the principle of dealing with people in the society which posits: "Take kindliness and benevolence as its basis, take frankness and friendliness as its bosom." If so, they will find out that not only will no counteraction be found in the mode of qigong they learned before but it will be enhanced instead.

Can Pan Gu Mystical Qigong be taught by others without approval?

Without Master Ou's approval you are unable to carry the directional information. Thus, the teaching effect will be influenced. Moreover, without his approval, when you teach others to exercise the *gong*, your own vitality will flow out unconsciously, and your own qi power will be weakened.

What are the qi sensations?

When the exercisers are in gong-posture (exercising or receiving *qi*), they may detect some sensations such as swelling, tingling, cold, heat, pain, itching, or they may feel a stream of air flowing in their body. These sensations are called *qi*-sensations. Strong or weak sensations vary from person to person as the biological field of each person differs. Therefore, whether *gong*-exercising is effective is not measured by having *qi*-sensations, or lack thereof. Someone may detect *qi*-sensations prior to his recovery, while others may recover their health before they detect *qi* sensations. No matter what may be, it is good to be comfortable, healthy.

Will any deviation appear in Pan Gu Mystical Qigong?

No deviation will appear in Pan Gu Mystical Qigong. Since the tenet of Pan Gu Mystical Qigong is formulated according to the feature of the physiological structure of the human body and the characteristic of the relationship between man and nature. Therefore, Pan Gu Mystical Qigong can only absorb the energy and the material elements that are beneficial to the human body, and bring good effect without any ill influence.

How do you explain the indisposition or pains which may appear during qigong exercise?

When practicing Pan Gu Mystical Qigong, you absorb material elements and energy from the Universe that are beneficial to the human body and which produce collision against elements of the disease in certain parts in your body. As a result, you may experience a feeling of indisposition or pain. This is the manifestation of the effect of exercising the *gong*. So long as you persist in your practice, the beneficial material elements and energy will be accumulated and strengthened in your body, the curative effects will be obtained, and the indisposed feelings will disappear.

Why doesn't Pan Gu Mystical Qigong advocate violent unconscious auto-moving gong?

Though the auto-moving *qi* produced in *gong*-exercising may disperse some disease elements, it will consume the real *qi* in the body. Attention should particularly be paid to the fact that someone may happen to be out of self-control during violent unconscious auto-movement. If it goes on continually, it will do great harm to the health, even bringing deviations. So it is not advisable to do violent self-unconscious moving.

How should we cognize and deal with the phenomena of penetrating vision and telepathic perceptive functions in case they occur after gong exercising?

Actually, there is an extremely great potential energy within man which may be induced under specific, objective conditions. Qigong exercising is just one kind of specific objective condition which will excavate the potential energy in man's body. Therefore "penetrating vision" and "perception" functions which may appear owing to *gong*-exercising are in fact normal phenomena. While it is a good thing, attention should be paid to the following aspects:

1. The information displayed in the appearance of the "penetrating vision" and "perceptive" functions are found in variety—some may be unpleasant, indisposed. As such, the exercisers should be ready in thought, deal with them at ease, and not be afraid to enhance health and cultivation quality with reinforcing *gong*-exercising and deepening their understanding so as to obtain the adapting ability to these things.

2. When you use your qigong ability to treat others, the information obtained under the condition of functions will be brought about. A positive role should be affirmed, but sometimes information may not reflect wholly the intrinsic quality of things and matter. Thus, to analyze the information is required, and we should take the information only for reference and do the utmost to persuade the patients to be at ease, to enhance their confidence in overcoming hardship, and fighting against illness. Provided that the work is well done, then the patient's condition will take a favorable turn.

What is the cause of man's diseases?

Aside from the objective causes, after analyzing the physiological structure of the human body, there can be found two reasons why illness is brought about:

1) The organs in the human body will incur pathological changes, such as a lack of necessary material elements or superfluity of harmful material elements. These diseases are mostly parenchymal diseases, or may be called as matter attribution diseases.

2) The diseases caused by the decline or the obstruction in

various physiological functions in the body do not display themselves in parenchymal diseases, so they may be labeled as spiritual attribution diseases.

What is the tenet of Pan Gu Mystical Qigong in curing sickness?

When performing these qigong exercises, the exercisers absorb directly the material elements from the great nature to cure the diseases caused by the lack or superfluity of the matter elements, and also strengthen the physiological functions of the various organs in the human body so as to recover and maintain exuberant vitality.

What diseases can be cured by Pan Gu Mystical Qigong?

The tenet of Pan Gu Mystical Gong in curing sickness is drawn according to the cause of the disease. So, theoretically, it can treat all kinds of diseases. Up to now, with the exception of patients suffering from aids with whom we have not yet contacted and dealt, we have almost treated every kind of disease and have been largely successful. Pan Gu Mystical Qigong has a special curative effect on the diseases caused by heart trouble and immunity as well as a good effect on all kinds of chronic diseases. However, the effects at last depends on the exerciser's own effort.

When can the exercisers issue qi to cure another's sickness?

As soon as the exercisers have learned and exercised the qigong mode, they can issue *qi* to treat others. This is one of the outstanding features of Pan Gu Mystical Qigong. The crux to it is that the exercisers should bear a heart of love, of confidence, and of perseverance, and dare to engage in treating practices.

Can those who suffer from sickness themselves treat others?

To issue *qi* and treat another's sickness can not only reduce the pain and agony of others, while also enhancing the quality of the issuers' own body. Therefore, it is unnecessary to wait for the complete recovery of all sickness in the body before treating another's diseases. This is also decided by the key of the mode of Pan Gu Mystical Qigong.

How can one enhance as quickly as possible the quality of the body and the power of qigong?

Frequent practices should be done, which consists of five aspects: exercising practice, reading practice, curing sickness practice, practice of guiding other people, and the practice of conducting oneself in society. So long as the practitioners insist in *gong*-exercising, repeated reading, comprehending thoroughly their thought, devoting a heart of love actively, issuing *qi* to cure others' sickness as frequently as possible, guiding others actively of their own accord to be benevolent and kind, to be frank and friendly, to live pleasantly, to devote wholeheartedly to public duty, and to suit the other people, his body quality and *qi* power will be rapidly enhanced.

If during the process of the practitioner issuing qi to treat others' sickness he himself has an indisposed feeling, what should he do?

If the issuer of *qi* detects an indisposed feeling in the corresponding part of his own body when he is issuing-*gong* to treat others' sickness, it is due to the sick *qi* affecting his own body, which is a body perceptive function. Take it easy if this happens. The issuer can generally adopt the way of *gong*-exercising to get rid of the sick *qi* or he may just disregard it and broaden his mind. The sick *qi* will then vanish of its own accord, and the corresponding part of the issuer will be tempered and his *gong* ability will then be further enhanced.

How does one use qigong to treat others' sickness?

The most basic and effective way to issue qigong to treat others' sickness is to let the patient relax his body, and put his two palms upward, while silently reciting: "Take kindliness and benevolence as its basis, take frankness and friendliness as its bosom." Next, issue *qi* toward the palms of the patient with your hands and pray, hoping that the indisposed part of the patient would turn for the better, or be cured. The issuer may also repeat silently to himself: "Take kindliness and benevolence as its basis, take frankness and friendliness as its bosom," and "Speak with reason, treat people with courtesy, move others with emotion, act with result." Besides, he may issue *qi* directly at the patients' affected part. No matter what way he adopts, if only he permeates the thought of benevolence and friendliness, then a good curative effect will also be produced. It is important to dare practice.

What is the relationship between curing sickness with medicine and with qigong exercises?

There is no contradiction between the two. To cure sickness with medicine is to suit the remedy to the case, which is a visible replenishment, while to cure sickness with qigong exercises is not only to absorb the material elements from the nature, which are beneficial to the body, so as to gain the same curative effect as the medicine, but also to adjust the physiological function in the body, and to strengthen the vitality which is an invisible replenishment.

What kinds of concrete methods have practitioners of Pan Gu Mystical Qigong summed up in their practice?

The main point of view of Pan Gu Mystical Qigong in curing sickness and helping others is to strengthen the vitality of the patients and to replenish the lacking material elements in the body. At the same time, to emphatically mobilize positive factors of the conscious action and super conscious action of the patients. Therefore, the basic way should be:

1) First to repeat silently: "Take kindliness and benevolence as its basis; take frankness and friendliness as its bosom."

2) To issue *qi* through the hand pose. The issuer poses his hands toward the patient's hands or the indisposed part with the intention of strengthening the patient's life functions and replenishing the beneficial material elements.

3) To issue *qi* with pure intention. Those practitioners who

have gained experience in static exercises may adopt this way according to the condition. The intention is to replenish the vitality and the beneficial material elements to the patient's whole body or to the sick part with gold and silver lights.

4) To issue your *qi* together with the patients (here refers to those who have learned Pan Gu Mystical Qigong), or by collective exercising qigong. By this way, the issuer can help the patient to contact the real *qi* of the Universe more quickly and to enhance the effect of good information as well as to strengthen the feeling in *gong*-exercising of the patient and establish his confidence.

5) To issue *qi* by joining hands to adjust the body collectively. By this way, the issuers may take others' strong points and to make up each others' deficiencies and to strengthen the effect of the *qi* field.

6) To guide with words. The way to do this is to guide the patient to read the key of the *gong*-exercises silently then to make him relax himself and have the idea of gold and silver lights penetrating from head to feet into the his body.

What activities can the exercisers take part in after learning the qigong exercises prescribed herein? What advantages do the learners gain from them?

The learners should take part in the activities in groups or in regional part after learning the qigong exercises. By exchanging the experience of exercising *qi* and through collective qigong exercising, they will gain beneficial adjustments to their body. The collective activity will give free rein to collective force. The greater *qi* field is an important way to enhance the body as quickly as possible.

What is the best breadth of mind the exerciser should bear when exercising?

"Kind-hearted, peaceful mood, broad-minded" is the most ideal principle and way of exercising.

What is meant by "To work follows to believe, to work follows sincerity"?

Qigong is provided with both conscious action and super-conscious action. Therefore, many modes of qigong advocate "to work follows to believe, to work follows sincerity." In fact, it only realizes the feature of qigong's conscious action. So, "to believe" is emphasized, hoping it will bring into play a great effect on the patient's body.

However, Pan Gu Mystical Qigong holds that although it is necessary to gain the conscious action for coordinating, the effect produced by super-conscious action is greater. Therefore, the learners are allowed to bear a doubt in their minds when practicing the exercises, because Pan Gu Mystical Qigong possesses an effect to induce and stimulate man's super-conscious action. After having gained some effects through *gong*-exercising, the learners should more positively dispel their doubts and coordinate their conscious actions with super-conscious actions. Kind-heartedness, a peaceful mood, and broad-mindedness are the best ways to closely coordinate conscious action with super-conscious action and to give free rein to better effect *gong*-exercising.

How can one understand the mystic and fantastic phenomena narrating in the book The Path of Life?

The objective reality of things and matter is by no means non-existence before the cognition of mankind. Rather, it is its existence that leads their cognition. Therefore, one should cognize and examine with an objective attitude toward mystic things and matters. The things that have been proven to exist should be used to bring happiness to mankind, no matter how mystic and fantastic they are. One may free himself from belief or disbelief in the things and matters that have not yet been proven to exist for the time being, and it is better to treat and to deal with them with a tolerant attitude. If someone is willing to probe into it, it would certainly be better.

*Why should gong-exercising be combined with reading the book
The Path of Life?*

The Path of Life is the theoretical basis of Pan Gu Mystical
Qigong. Through reading and pondering, the learners can
deepen their comprehension of Pan Gu Mystical Qigong,
step by step. Reading practice can guide the learners in
gong-exercising and in sickness-curing, and can help the
learners in the practice of guiding others and in the practice of conducting oneself in society. "Practice is the basis,
theory is a short-cut, reading is a key." One more comprehension to a view-point will emerge an imperceptible
influence on one's quality of body and mind of their own
accord.

*How should one look upon the exceptional functions and the
extraordinary phenomena?*

Some exceptional functions, such as penetrating vision and
perceptions, may appear and some extraordinary phenomena, such as photism, phonism, hallucination may occur in
some students during gong-exercising. They are caused by
the fact that the latent energy of man is excavated and the
gradual acceptance of the information by man. Thus, they
are normal phenomena.

The appearance of exceptional functions and extraordinary
phenomena should be treated and analyzed properly. The
aim of *gong*-exercising is at cultivation both in flesh and
soul, and at enhancing the quality both in body and
thought. Therefore, we should not sedulously strive for the
exceptional functions and extraordinary phenomena.

Epilogue

Harmony Between Heaven, Earth, and Man

The Heaven rests with its spiritual emptiness; the Earth rests with its thick solidness. Once the Heaven and the Earth combine together, and there are spirit and its body, human beings can be brought up and matter substances made.

Man's spirit is like the Heaven and man's physical body is like the Earth. The spirit is the soul and thinking, and the body is the material substance. When harmony between the spirit and flesh is achieved, a perfect man is made. Man cannot live without matter, nor without spirit. Man is in his perfect condition only when his *qi* (energy) and *yi* (mind) are highly spirited and vigorous.

Qi is matter, while *yi* is spirit. *Qi* is both matter and spirit, primarily matter and secondarily spirit; while *yi* is both spirit and matter, primarily spirit and secondarily matter. *Qi* comes with *yi*, and *yi* generates from the heart. Only when a man's *qi* and *yi* combine into one, can he be a genuine man.

Exercise *yi* to lay a firm foundation; gather *qi* to keep the body fit. Free the mind from evil thoughts and qi will be good. Take in everything good, reinforce the root, trace it to the source, eliminate diseases, keep fit, and live longer. Retribution for good or evil can surely be found in how one is tempered.

As the sun homologizes the moon, so *yin* achieves balance with *yang*—it has opened up a path for all things on Earth to live and multiply in peace. Be kind and friendly, accumulate virtues and do good deeds, and the human race is on its bright road to the future.

The Universe will never become extinct, neither will its matter. But why is man mortal? It is because man is unable to achieve harmony with the everlasting Universe and its existent matter.

Harmony is in fact cooperation, and close coexistence. Therefore, if one tempers oneself both spiritually and physically, one should be able to live forever. This is not false.

For those interested in attending a formal Pan Gu Mystical Qigong class, or would like more information on Pan Gu Mystical Qigong or the book, *The Path of Life*, feel free to contact Master Ou Wen Wei at the following address:

Pan Gu Shengong Int'l Research Institute
569 Geary Street, Suite 200
San Francisco, CA 94102
(415) 928-1389

Reference Guide

Figure 1

Figure 2

Figure 3

Figure 7

Figure 8

Figure 9

Figure 12

Figure 13

Figure 4   Figure 5   Figure 6

Figure 10   Figure 11

Figure 14